Called Out
Kaleo Academy Workbook

Derek Brown, Ph.D.
Director of Theological Studies
Kaleo Academy

KALEO ACADEMY

The purpose of Kaleo Academy is to identify and build the capacity of high-leadership potential Quaker youth for future ministry and service positions in the Friends Church. Kaleo Academy participants will explore historical Quaker writings and the Christian Scriptures and consider how they speak into the ethical and moral dimensions of contemporary social issues. Reflecting on Quaker faith and practice, as expressed in the evangelical Friends tradition, participants will consider how these inform their decisions about life purpose and calling and future vocation. They will also develop attitudes and intentions that lead to thoughtful consideration and active pursuit of full-time ministry and religious leadership.

CONTENTS

HOW TO USE THIS BOOK

This workbook is meant to be used at Theology Camp and throughout the year. The first part of the book contains pages to write down notes from the class session of Theology Camp. The rest of the book contains the monthly sessions corresponding to the sessions at camp. <u>Working with your mentor</u>, you will read through and answer the questions each month. You will then be required to post one or more of your answers in the online classroom (further instructions will be given).

THEOLOGY CAMP NOTES

The first section of this book contains lined pages for you to take notes on during the classroom sessions of Theology Camp. This is an easy way to keep your notes for the entire week together in one place, so you can refer back to them throughout the year. Plus, studies have shown that writing notes by hand actually improves memory and understanding. Finally, your instructors have invested time and energy into their lessons, because they believe in you and want to help you succeed in your walk with Christ. You want to make sure you collect their wisdom and insight, so that it may benefit you, both now and in the future.

SESSION SECTIONS

Each session section will begin with a short devotional that highlights a specific topic of the session. This is meant to help you both understand the topic, as well as get you into the right frame of mind for answering the reflection questions.

PERSONAL PRACTICE

The goal of Kaleo Academy is to prepare and equip you for service, leadership, and ministry, in the Church and in the world. We, and the churches who sent you, recognize your giftings and potential, and we want to do all we can to help sharpen and deepen your faith, so that you may be prepared to do God's work – whenever, wherever, and whatever that may be. Above all, we want to sharpen your faith, and deepen your walk with Christ

The Personal Practice element of each session section provides the opportunity to further think about the concepts and issues of each session, along with questions that help you put the knowledge into practice.

CHURCH CONNECTION

The "Church Connection" piece of each session section helps connect the session content with your community of faith. Although you may never "work" in the Church as an employee, you will and should be serving (volunteering) in your church. Just as the Personal Practice helps deepen your walk with Christ, the Church Connection will help you better see the great things your church is doing, as well as the opportunities for you to use your gifts to bless the Body of Christ.

BIGGER PICTURE

Part of the Kaleo experience is the "Released Project." The following definition can be found in your Released Project Handbook:

The Kaleo Academy Released Project is an opportunity to see God use a student in specific ways he may be the them (in their local community, church, yearly meeting, or around the world). Early Friends would call those going out into ministry "Released Ministers." We want to use this opportunity to release this young generation of Friends leaders into ministry in the church, communities and the world. For the Released Project, students will partner with your pastoral leaders and their Mentor in finding an effective service learning project (it could be organized like an internship). The goals is for students to pick a Released Project that fits both the needs of their community and utilizes their gifts and calling. Students will contribute at least 50 hours toward this project during your year in Kaleo Academy.

The instructions and details of the project can be founded in the Released Project handbook. The purpose of the Bigger Picture questions are to help you think about this project in a prayerful, Christ-centered manner. The Bigger Picture portion of each session section will help situate the Released Project within the broader context of the Kingdom of God, as well as helping your record/track the personal growth you will experience during this process.

MENTOR BLESSING

This last section is for the mentor/mentee to write a blessing in each other's books. This is a chance to compliment and thank each other for the meetings, prayers, and journey you have had together over the past year. Above all, it is a memory marking beginning of a mentoring friendship that will, hopefully, continue for years to come.

THEOLOGY CAMP NOTES

INTRODUCTION TO
BIBLICAL INTERPRETATION

Session One

How can a young person stay on the path of purity? By living according to your word.
(Psalm 119:9)

George Fox dedicated his life to the study of Scripture. As a teenager, he would often travel into the country to read the Bible and pray. It was during these travels that he had a revelation that he could have a relationship with Jesus Christ, right here and right now – without any empty ritual standing between them. George Fox was filled with joy, and dedicated the rest of his life to spreading this Good News.

Fox's preaching and writing were filled with references to Scripture. He wrote nearly 3000 letters in his lifetime, and although he wasn't the best writer (he was terrible actually – so if you think you can't write well - don't be discouraged – God will still use you!), his writings were saturated with the Word of God. This overflow of Scripture did not occur overnight, but after many years of reading the Bible daily.

I am sure most of you would love to have that same familiarity and consistent presence of the Bible in your life. However, there are two typical obstacles that prevent this: life feels too busy and/or you don't know how to begin. While life will always be busy, it is important to make time to read the prayerfully read the Bible. The good news is that there is an easy way to methodically introduce it into your daily life.

Try this. I want you to read the Bible for one minute a day, and pray for one minute a day. That is it. Then, the following week, try to read for two minutes a day and pray for two minutes a day. Keeping increasing, one minute at a time, week after week. Some of you may already read and pray more than that - I still ask that you set your timer and try this method - I bet that, little by little, each of you will build a consistent, daily habit of Word and prayer.

PERSONAL PRACTICE

Do you make time to pray and read the Bible? If so, how often? If not, why not?

_____

_____

_____

_____

_____

What are the biggest obstacles/challenges, in your life, to prayer and the study of God's Word?

_____

_____

_____

_____

_____

_____

_____

_____

_____

_____

_____

Look over the "little by little" Bible reading method described above. Is this something you will try? Why or why not? If not, how will introduce/increase prayer and Bible study into your daily life?

_____

_____

_____

_____

_____

_____

_____

_____

_____

_____

_____

_____

_____

_____

_____

_____

_____

CHURCH CONNECTION

Ask three members of your church about their habits of prayer and Bible reading in their daily life. Ask them for advice about creating habits in your life. Record their answers below:

_____

_____

_____

_____

_____

_____

_____

_____

_____

_____

_____

_____

_____

_____

_____

_____

_____

_____

BIGGER PICTURE

The foundation of your Released Project should be a relationship with Jesus Christ. Read Matthew 7:21-23:

> *Not everyone who says to me, 'Lord, Lord,' will enter the kingdom of heaven, but only the one who does the will of my Father who is in heaven. Many will say to me on that day, 'Lord, Lord, did we not prophesy in your name and in your name drive out demons and in your name perform many miracles?' Then I will tell them plainly, 'I never knew you. Away from me, you evildoers!'*

With your mentor, answer the following questions:

Why did the people think they deserved to enter the kingdom of heaven?

_____

_____

_____

_____

What were they missing? Why did their ministry and miracles mean nothing?

_____

_____

_____

_____

_____

_____

_____

_____

As you begin thinking about your Released Project, what is this verse teaching you?

_____

_____

_____

_____

_____

_____

_____

_____

_____

_____

_____

_____

_____

_____

_____

_____

_____

_____

HISTORICAL QUAKER FAITH AND PRACTICE

Session One

Do not conform to the pattern of this world, but be transformed by the renewing of your mind. Then you will be able to test and approve what God's will is--his good, pleasing and perfect will.
(Romans 12:2)

But small is the gate and narrow the road that leads to life, and only a few find it.
(Matthew 7:14)

One way to understand the Quaker testimonies is as a conviction to be obedient to God, no matter the cost. An example of this can be found in North Carolina Quaker history. There is a story told about a wealthy family of tobacco growers who wanted to fund a school founded by Quakers and Methodists. However, the Quakers, not wanting to accept money earned from tobacco sales, declined. The Methodists accepted, however, and the family continued to pour money into the school, which was soon named after the family – Duke University![1] The Quakers' convictions cost them a lot of money, yet they would not compromise their obedience to the Lord.

It is not always easy to be a faithful Christian in today's world. Even though we have given our lives to Christ, inherited eternal life, and are filled with the Holy Spirit – we still must daily resist the temptations of this world – temptations to compromise, to sin, and to reject the teachings of Scripture and the leading of the Holy Spirit. There will be points in your life where you will feel that you are the only one around who is trying to live for God, and you may stumble more times than you can imagine. Obedience is often costly.

However, a life lived in obedience to God is a life that is truly blessed. The best way to live in obedience is to recognize that there is no other time that matters but the present moment. Each and every minute you have the opportunity to either live for God....or not. If you stumble, it's okay, for it is in the past, and there is no other time that matters but the present. Try to recognize that life is a series of moments – so make the most of them.

PERSONAL PRACTICE

To help better understand the distinctive testimonies of Quakerism in the context of our walk with Jesus, you and your mentor should take each of the Quaker testimonies (Simplicity, Peace, Integrity, Community, Equality) and do the following things:

Find one passage of Scripture which supports/explains each one (if you can find a passage that has Jesus explaining/commanding it, all the better).

Simplicity

_____

_____

_____

_____

Peace

_____

_____

_____

_____

Integrity

_____

_____

_____

_____

Community

_____

_____

_____

_____

Equality

_____

_____

_____

Give an example of how you can live out these commands of Christ (testimonies) in your daily life.

Simplicity

_____

_____

_____

_____

_____

_____

_____

Peace

_____

_____

_____

_____

Integrity

_____

_____

_____

Community

_____

_____

_____

Equality

_____

_____

_____

_____

CHURCH CONNECTION

If possible, interview your pastor and ask the following questions (write their answers below):

Which of the Quaker testimonies (Simplicity, Peace, Integrity, Community, Equality) is most important? Why?

_____

_____

_____

_____

_____

_____

Does our church excel in any one of these testimonies? How?

_____

_____

_____

_____

_____

_____

_____

_____

How does living a lifestyle of obedience to the commands of Jesus (like the testimonies) help communicate the Gospel to non-believers?

_____

_____

_____

_____

_____

_____

_____

_____

_____

_____

_____

_____

_____

_____

_____

_____

_____

_____

BIGGER PICTURE

Even though Quakerism was a small Christian movement, it had a big impact, for its followers were faithful and obedient to God's commands and His call on their lives. In order to help you ground your Released Project in the historic framework of Quakerism, please answer the following:

If you have a basic idea for your outreach project - which testimony would it fall under? Why?

_____

_____

_____

_____

_____

If you don't have an idea yet - which testimony most interests you? Why?

_____

_____

_____

_____

_____

_____

_____

_____

_____

CONTEMPORARY SOCIAL ISSUES AND FRIENDS FAITH AND PRACTICE

Session One

In the last days, God says, I will pour out my Spirit on all people.
Your sons and daughters will prophesy...
(Joel 2:28)

There is neither Jew nor Gentile, neither slave nor free, nor is there male and female, for
you are all one in Christ Jesus.
(Galatians 3:28)

One of the earliest examples of the Quaker testimony of equality is through the empowerment of women to preach and minister. It is hard to imagine how radical this was in the culture of seventeenth-century England. Women were not viewed as equal to men, but instead looked upon as weak and inferior, and even the laws of England were based on this idea. Spiritually, women were also viewed as inferior; there were even some who believed that women did not have a soul, "no more than a goose," which is not very nice.[2] The common opinion was that women could not be ministers – no exceptions.

Quakers sent shockwaves through society by believing that men and women were equal instruments of God, to be used to spread the Gospel through the world. The result was something never seen in Christianity – women preachers and missionaries traveling throughout England and to foreign lands, preaching the Good News of Jesus Christ. One minister, Mary Fisher, even traveled from England to Turkey to preach to the Sultan of the Ottoman Empire![3] In the local churches, Quaker women led their own meetings, oversaw and approved marriages, and helped those in need. Many of these Quaker women have not been remembered; instead it has been the Quaker men that people know about today. Back then, however, female Quaker ministers were celebrities, and recognized as much as the men. In fact, one poem equated Quaker minister Rachel Wilson (who is unknown today) to John Woolman (the famed Quaker abolitionist): "That like a Woolman or Wilson shines."[4]

Without God using Quakerism to empower these female ministers, they may have never listened for or obeyed the calling of God into ministry. What impact has the Church lost because some of its members do not feel empowered to follow the calling God has laid on their hearts? One of the reasons to strive for the biblical concept of equality is because when all people feel equal and unified in the Body of Christ, then everyone can utilize their gifts freely and boldly, helping expand the Kingdom of God.

PERSONAL PRACTICE

In both the Old and the New Testament, it is very clear that God loves and favors those that world rejects - the marginalized of society (what we would call "outcasts"). Part of our walk with Christ means stepping outside of our zone of friends and seeing/treating others as Christ would, and helping others see in themselves what God sees in them. By treating all with equal respect, we empower people to have an identity free from insecurity and fear, so that they may ultimately find their true identity in Christ.

This is so incredibly important in high school, where cliques form, social castes exist, and those deemed "outcasts" are either invisible or are bullied. Because of social pressures, it can be difficult to treat others with love and respect (especially if they are mean to you). Thinking about this, answer the following questions:

What is one concrete way that you can act towards others at school that reflects the love of God?

_____

_____

_____

_____

What keeps you from treating all students with the same kindness, respect, and care that you would treat your friends?

_____

_____

_____

_____

_____

_____

CHURCH CONNECTION

You may not realize how much your church does to help others, both locally and abroad. Looking at the bulletin, church website, or asking others, find out what your church is doing to be the light of Christ to the world. List what you find - is there a ministry or service that interests you? If there is, who would go and talk to about it?

_____

_____

_____

_____

_____

_____

_____

_____

_____

_____

_____

_____

_____

_____

BIGGER PICTURE

As Quakers sought to bring justice and shalom to the world around them, their work occurred through a holy sensitivity to the needs of their community. In the same way, your Released Project should address a need in your community. In the Released Project handbook, it states:

> While planning, and preparing, you should meet with leadership in your local church assembly on a regular basis. Whether that is in the church building itself, a restaurant, or a coffee shop. Your church leadership will be the ones to help point you in the right directions in order for you to obtain the right tools needed to complete your Released Project.

In the space below, write out your notes and reflections on your meeting with the leadership of your community of faith.

_____

_____

_____

_____

_____

_____

_____

_____

_____

_____

_____

_____

CHRISTIAN LEADERSHIP

Session One

Show yourself in all respects to be a model of good works, and in your teaching show integrity, dignity, and sound speech that cannot be condemned, so that an opponent may be put to shame, having nothing evil to say about us.
(Titus 2:7-8)

The main message of the Christian Leadership session is that leadership is influence. When you influence others, you are practicing leadership. Even if you do not have a position of leadership (e.g. coach, principal, manager, boss, etc.), you can still lead people by virtue of your influence. How so? Through your actions and attitudes, your life is broadcasting influence. You have the opportunity to change how people think, feel, and act by simply being an example for others to follow.

John Woolman was an American Quaker who lived in the 18th-century. He became convicted that slavery was wrong and that it should be abolished in the United States (this was almost 100 years before the Civil War). However, he was a simple merchant, and it appeared unlikely that he could have great effect on society. Regardless, his actions broadcasted his conviction.

As part of his work, he was often asked to write out people's wills. He refused to do so, though, if the person was a slave-owner who was passing on their slaves as inheritance. While this upset the slave-owners, it planted a seed of God's truth in their minds, and there were occasions where slave-owners repented and agreed to free their slaves (Woolman was happy to write out their will then!).[5] When he traveled on a missionary journey to the American South, he walked, so that the slaves at the places where he stayed would not have extra work caring for his horse. Also, at those places, he would pay the slaves for their services (which was taken as an insult by the hosts). While, on the surface, these actions don't seem like they would have an impact, it was the consistent influence of Woolman's lifestyle that helped propel Quakerism to eventually free all of the slaves held by its members.

Your actions and attitudes, no matter great or small, have influence. You may never realize it, but the example you set may change a life, a church, a community, or perhaps even the nation. Woolman did not set out to change society, he merely lived out his convictions with the hope that he could change the minds of the few people he came into contact with. If you want to be a great Christian leader, helping transform the world in the name of Jesus, begin by living out your convictions, with the prayerful hope that you can be the catalyst for change in the people around you.

PERSONAL PRACTICE

Who do you know that exemplifies Christian Leadership? Why?

_____

_____

_____

_____

_____

_____

What are some ways you are using your influence to lead in a Christ-like manner? How can you do this more effectively?

_____

_____

_____

_____

_____

_____

_____

_____

_____

CHURCH CONNECTION

If leadership is influence, then the best way a church can be a leading presence in the community is through its influence – being the "salt and light" (Mt. 5:13-16). Sometimes we don't realize the influence our churches have on the world around us. Through our outreach programs, evangelism, service to the poor and needy, and funding/sending of missionaries around the world - the local church can have a big impact.

However, some say that Church tries to do too much, and ends up having a bunch of programs and ministries that never reach their full potential. Instead, they say, the church should choose one or two key ministries and focus on them. Think about this, discuss with others, and answer the following question:

The local church should only focus on one or two ministries/programs/outreach initiatives, instead of a bunch of different ones. Do you agree or disagree? Why? (In case you are worried – there is no objective right/wrong answer – just asking for your opinion.)

_____

_____

_____

_____

_____

_____

_____

_____

_____

_____

If leadership is influence, how is your church leading?

_____

_____

_____

_____

_____

_____

_____

_____

_____

_____

_____

_____

_____

_____

_____

_____

_____

BIGGER PICTURE

One of the Released Project milestones is to identify two possible project ideas. List and explain the two possibilities below, including why you chose them.

_____

_____

_____

_____

_____

_____

_____

_____

_____

_____

_____

_____

_____

_____

_____

_____

_____

CALLED OUT

CALLING AND VOCATION

Session One

Is not wisdom found among the aged? Does not long life bring understanding?
(Job 12:12)

The geographer and biologist Jared Diamond tells a story about when he was researching on a remote island in the South Pacific. There he met an old woman (perhaps in her eighties) who was the only person on the island who had lived through the last cyclone (one that ravaged the island). On that island, she was the only person who knew which fruit, roots, and other food sources could be eaten in an emergency (like when a cyclone destroys all the gardens and food supplies). She was respected for her wisdom and knowledge, for "if another cyclone were to strike...her encyclopedic memory of which wild fruits to eat would be all that stood between her fellow villagers and starvation."[6]

While perhaps not about wild fruits and vegetables, the older people in your life do have a lot of valuable knowledge and wisdom – especially regarding spirituality and faith. Yet it may be difficult for you to go up and talk to older people – even if they attend the same church as you. If you feel this way, you are not alone. It is something that is quite common, and it has affected the Church is some serious ways.

One of the main issues facing the Church is the division between age groups (young people, adults, elderly). Christian anthropologist Margaret Mead wrote that cultures pass on important information when three generations (young, adult, elderly) interact.[7] This holds true for churches, which are healthiest when the young, the adults, and the elderly worship, fellowship, and serve together. However, some churches focus only on young people, while others focus only on older members. A healthy church will not only have all three groups present during worship, but also interacting in each other's lives. Followers of Jesus should seek to interact and get to know other people in their church, regardless of their age or background.

In the Bible, wisdom is associated with age. This is because those who are older have experienced more, and have learned from mistakes, setbacks, tragedies, successes and adventures. However, this wisdom is often untapped as older people are not often asked to share their story. As you think about your direction in life (what God may be calling you to) it can be very helpful to hear the life stories of others - their decisions, struggles, calling, and vocation. Hearing the (often amazing) stories of older people can help provide you with wisdom, tips, and inspiration.

However, as a teenager, it may be intimidating to get to know "old" people (even though they are delighted that you belong to the church and often are praying for you). So the following assignment should not only to achieve the aims of "Calling and Vocation," but also to help build and strengthen some relationships you have in the church.

PERSONAL PRACTICE

Find at least one member of your church who is over the age of 70 (or 60 is there is no one over 70). Ask them if they would be willing to sit down and talk with you sometime. When you do meet, ask to hear their story about their life. Be patient and just listen. Use the space below to write down notes during the interview.

CHURCH CONNECTION

There may be some of you who will be called into a ministry position (pastor, missionary, etc.). This is a momentous decision, and one not to be taken lightly. Whether or not you think you will ever go into full-time ministry, it would be beneficial to hear from those who have responded to that calling. Ask someone in a ministry position if they would tell you the story of their calling and response. Write your notes below:

_____

_____

_____

_____

_____

_____

_____

_____

_____

_____

_____

_____

_____

_____

_____

BIGGER PICTURE

Think about your own story so far and how God has shaped it. Find your S.H.A.P.E. profile from Theology Camp. Spend some time this month with your mentor praying over your S.H.A.P.E. profile and reviewing what themes or insights come from it. Then come up with 2 words or phrases that describe your story so far and record them below. Have fun!

How is God shaping your story?

_____

_____

_____

_____

_____

_____

_____

_____

_____

_____

_____

_____

_____

_____

INTRODUCTION TO BIBLICAL INTERPRETATION

Session Two

For unto us a Child is born,
Unto us a Son is given;
And the government will be upon His shoulder.
And His name will be called
Wonderful, Counselor, Mighty God,
Everlasting Father, Prince of Peace.
(Isaiah 9:6-7)

As you enjoy the Christmas season, with its sense of mystery and possibility, I want you to recognize that salvation, offered to the whole world, came about because of the obedience of a teenage couple – most likely around your age. Joseph was probably around 17-18, while Mary was between 14-16. Imagine the courage it would take for them to be faithful. Mary was to carry the Lord's child, while suffering the anger and accusations of her family (their daughter pregnant before marriage – a very shameful event in that culture). Joseph, who thought Mary had cheated on him, was ready to move on and never speak to her again. When the angel commanded him to raise the child as his own, Joseph had to let go of his feelings of betrayal, anger, and doubt, and accept Mary as his wife and Jesus as his son. Both of them had to endure life in the small town of Nazareth, whose townspeople, because they did not know the truth, viewed this pregnancy as a scandal – just some irresponsible teenagers lacking the self-control to wait until marriage. For Mary and Joseph, following the will of God took courage and sacrifice.

What is amazing is that God put the birth of the Messiah, his own son, in the hands of two teenagers. Some may ask why God would place something so important into the hands of two people who are too young and inexperienced? Perhaps God does not view people in the same way, for maybe age, gender, race, intelligence (or any number of things) has nothing to do with how God uses people to accomplish his will. Perhaps it is simply faith and obedience – the two key traits that Mary and Joseph possessed – that made them worthy partners with God to bring about the salvation of the world. Perhaps that is all we need, and what we should be striving for?

Remember, if God could do such world-changing things through a baby born in a cave, to teenage parents in a backwoods country town.....what great things could he also do through you?

PERSONAL PRACTICE

Part of interpreting a narrative (story) passage of Scripture is understanding the characters, context, and situations found in the passage. In other words, put yourself in the shoes of the characters – what were they thinking? What were they feeling? What are the sights, sounds, and smells in the scene? If you were there, what would you do?

Read Luke 2:8-20, the story of the shepherds in the fields of Bethlehem, who get to be the first to witness the birth of the Son of God. Using your imagination, place yourself in the story, and describe the scene, using the questions in the first paragraph.

_____

_____

_____

_____

_____

_____

_____

_____

_____

_____

_____

_____

_____

_____

Record any insights or thoughts about the shepherds' story that you gained from the exercise above.

_____

_____

_____

_____

_____

The shepherds were such lower-class outsiders that, even though they were present at the Incarnation, it would have been easy for Luke to have left them out of the story (just like a TV show doesn't focus on the garbage truck going down the street behind the main characters; it is just in the background, and forgettable). The fact that their story is told means that God wanted us to know their story. Why do think the shepherds' story is important for us to know?

_____

_____

_____

_____

_____

_____

_____

_____

CHURCH CONNECTION

The Church offers many ways to learn about God (e.g. lessons, small groups, etc.) but, historically, the primary method used by the Church was music - and this is especially true during Christmas. Christmas carols/songs/hymns, which were written to be sung together as a community/family of God, have taught many about the glory of the Incarnation. Look at the lyrics of your favorite Christmas carol and answer the following questions:

What is the song? Why did you choose this song?

_____

_____

_____

_____

_____

What is the message of the song?

_____

_____

_____

_____

_____

_____

_____

Looking at the lyrics, is there anything you have noticed that you haven't before?

_____

_____

_____

_____

_____

Is there anything in the lyrics that you don't understand or have a question about?

_____

_____

_____

_____

_____

_____

_____

_____

_____

_____

_____

_____

BIGGER PICTURE

Choose your Released Project idea and brainstorm ways to implement the project.

_____

_____

_____

_____

_____

_____

_____

_____

_____

_____

_____

_____

_____

_____

_____

_____

Write down a list of people who could help you complete this Released Project.

_____

_____

_____

_____

_____

_____

_____

_____

_____

_____

_____

_____

_____

_____

_____

_____

HISTORICAL QUAKER FAITH AND PRACTICE

Session Two

Yet a time is coming and has now come when the true worshipers will worship the Father in the Spirit and in truth, for they are the kind of worshipers the Father seeks.
(John 4:23)

If you Google the painting "The Presence in the Midst," by Doyle Penrose, you will see a traditional Quaker worship service. Quaker worship was known for its silence, which was interrupted by people standing to share something God had laid on their hearts.

The presence of Jesus communicates that Christ is the one speaking through each of them, as well as the fulfillment of Matthew 18:20, "*Where two or three are gathered in my name, there I am with them.*" Be encouraged by this: whenever you pray with someone, or go to youth group, or sit in church - the presence and blessing of God is there too!

What made Quaker worship distinctive is that, as long as they were led by God, anyone could share. It didn't matter if they were young, old, man, woman, etc. All were free to speak. However, in spite of everyone participating, it was still important to have order in service. This quote by Quaker John Banks, in the 17th century, shows this:

"In all your meetings together to do service for the Lord, his truth, and people, and to see that good order be kept in the churches of Christ, wait diligently to be endowed with power and wisdom from above..."

Unity, order, obedience, and participation. These were key facets of early Quaker worship. As current kingdom-builders and future leaders of the Church, imagine a future where everyone feels the freedom to be obedient to God in worship – an obedience that leads to truth spoken, people edified and encouraged, and the congregation convicted to be the salt and light of the earth.

PERSONAL PRACTICE

It is very easy for people to criticize the Church, especially the worship service. While there are ways we could change what a church service looks like (see Church Connection), we must first shine the spotlight on ourselves.

Looking back at the past 6 months, how often did you attend your local church?

_____

_____

What are the biggest obstacles, for you, to church attendance?

_____

_____

_____

_____

Now, church attendance does not determine whether or not you are a "good" Christian. But the Christian life is meant to be lived in community. In your opinion, why is being a part of a community of faith so important?

_____

_____

_____

_____

_____

_____

CHURCH CONNECTION

One of the main fears of allowing everyone to participate in worship is that things will get out of control (can you remember a time when things got chaotic in youth group?). Thinking about this, post your opinion about this question:

In your church, if you were in charge, how would you change the worship service so that everyone would have a chance to participate?

_____

_____

_____

_____

_____

_____

_____

_____

_____

_____

_____

_____

_____

_____

_____

_____

BIGGER PICTURE

Unfortunately, it is typically to feel, because you are younger, that you are not ready or too young to lead your Released Project. I want to encourage you to recognize that God brought you to Kaleo for many reasons, one of which is to go back to your home church to make an impact.

Take some time to read, think, and pray about 1 Timothy 4:12:

> *Don't let anyone look down on you because you are young, but set an example for the believers in speech, in conduct, in love, in faith and in purity.*

Below, record your thoughts – what is God trying to tell you through this verse?

_____

_____

_____

_____

_____

_____

_____

_____

_____

_____

_____

_____

Contemporary Social Issues and Friends Faith And Practice

Session Two

Let us not become weary in doing good, for at the proper time we will reap a harvest if we do not give up.
(Galatians 6:9)

Dwight Moody is one of the most famous preachers in the history of American Christianity. Though he lived and preached in the 1800s, and did not have the benefit of technology and mass communication to spread his message, some say that, by the time he died, he had preached to over 100 million people.[8] His legacy is seen today in the Moody Bible Institute – a Bible college that trains Christians to impact the world for Christ. He dedicated his life to reaching the lost and preaching the Gospel of Jesus Christ.

What is surprising is that, when you look at his personal letters and articles from his local newspaper, you realize that the greatest impact he had on his community may have been his gardening! Moody spent a lot of time working in his garden, as well as planting trees and shrubs in his community. He would give away the fruit and vegetables from his garden, which helped feed a dozen or so families in his town.[9] Now, giving away fruit and vegetables from a small garden may not seem like a big deal, especially when compared to preaching the Gospel to 100 million people. However, when he died, it was this act of generosity that was the focus of the newspaper's obituary for him.

Do not worry about making a big impact in this world. Instead, focus on seeking first the kingdom of God, and serving others with a Christ-like attitude. When you do this, you will realize that, even when you do small things – because you are doing them in Jesus' name – they become great things. The smallest act of kindness can change the world, so let's pray that we can be aware of all the ways we can preach the Gospel through our life and actions.

PERSONAL PRACTICE

This session focuses on how we, as the Body of Christ on earth, can partner with God in proclaiming the "good news" of Christ Jesus, and seek to help those who are marginalized and in need (as we see from Jesus' example).

However, one can be overwhelmed by the size of the problems in this world, and become discouraged in the face of suffering, sadness, and evil. Many have asked themselves if they could make a dent in even one of the issues humanity faces. Because many followers of Christ don't know what to do, or how to begin, they do nothing.

I often felt that way. However, I came across a statement some time ago, and it has dramatically changed the way I approach the issues of this world:

DO FOR ONE WHAT YOU WISH YOU COULD DO FOR ALL

You may not be able to end world hunger, but you could buy a sandwich for the homeless person you pass by on the street. You may not be able to erase bullying, but you can stand up for those in your school who are bullied.

If every Christian did for one what they wish they could do for all, I truly believe the world would be changed.

Answer the following questions:

What can I do for one that I wish I could do for all? Is God laying anything on your heart? What are the first steps I need to take to do this? Are there any conversations I need to have?

_____

_____

_____

_____

CHURCH CONNECTION

Your church may not be very large, nor have lots of money, but it does have something incredibly valuable - believers who are filled with the Holy Spirit and the love of Christ. By doing for some what it wishes it could do for all, a church can change lives, transform communities, and help point people to the life-saving power of the Gospel.

What can my church do for some that I wish we could do for everyone?

_____

_____

_____

_____

_____

_____

_____

_____

_____

_____

_____

_____

_____

_____

BIGGER PICTURE

As mentioned above, we should not worry about seeking great results, but rather be faithful in our daily actions and interactions with others. Remember, while Jesus bought salvation for all of humanity with his sacrifice, he did not sprint to the cross, ignoring everything else in order to get the greatest return on his investment. Rather, Jesus never hesitated to meet with, heal, and forgive people, even people who were forgotten by society and "worth nothing."

Likewise, we should not measure the impact of our actions and ministry according to the world's terms, but recognize that, in God's "economy" (the word comes from the Greek meaning "household" - thus, God's household) even the smallest actions can have great impact.

Working with your mentor, answer the following question about your Released Project:

"What needs to happen for me to consider this project a success?"

Remember, success should not be measured by the world's standards. However, in answering this question, you and your mentor will articulate the most important goal of your project, as well ensuring that you are looking at your Released Project with a "God's-eye view," and not measuring it by worldly standards. Write down your answer below:

_____

_____

_____

_____

_____

_____

_____

CHRISTIAN LEADERSHIP

Session Two

Then I heard the voice of the Lord saying, "Whom shall I send? And who will go for us?" And I said, "Here am I. Send me!"
(Isaiah 6:8)

"Keychain leadership," a concept found in the book *Growing Young* by Kara Powell, Jake Mulder, and Brad Griffin, imagines positions and responsibilities in the church as "keys" – a symbol representing power and authority (as a key opens a door).[10] Just like someone holding a key, the person in that leadership role should feel empowered to invest themselves in their ministry. However, the leader should also be ready to "hand over the key" to a new person ready and able to take over that position. This way, the important ministries of the church never collapse after the loss of a leader, and the next generation of leaders are allowed to invest and utilize their gifts.

However, this is often not what happens in the local church. Oftentimes, positions in the church are given to whoever is willing to volunteer, and because many churches are thankful just to find a person to fill the spot, they often don't communicate the empowerment and responsibility required of each volunteer. In this, the Church needs to repent, and begin empowering young people with ministry opportunities and responsibilities. By willingly "handing over the key," the Church has the opportunity to infuse its ministries with energy, vision, and potential.

But this is also a two-way street. For a church to empower young adults into leadership positions, young adults have to be ready and willing to step into those responsibilities. Ideally, if you want to grow into a leadership position, people should already be able to see your commitment and service in the "little things." Also, while it may feel good to be offered a chance to be a "leader," you must make sure you never jump into a role because of pride, or a desire to have power and respect. That will not only end of damaging that ministry but, more important, may damage you spiritually. Remember, God wants to use you, but not at the cost of losing you.

At the end of the day, if you feel the Lord leading you into greater service in your local church, and the opportunity is given, we pray that you would have the courage to say "Here am I, send me!"

PERSONAL PRACTICE

The issue of pride is a topic worth exploring further. A person's greatest weakness can be pride, for it blinds them to the reality of the situation, including their own weaknesses. In early Quakerism, when a young adult felt called to be a minister, they would often delay letting people know, so that he or she could be sure that this calling was from God, and not from pride or vanity. Sometimes they would wait for years (we do not recommend this)! It was that important to make sure they were not acting out of human weakness, but in God's power.

Take a moment to reflect – how vulnerable are you to pride? Using the space below, write out a prayer to God, asking Him to give you the humility, wisdom, and strength to serve Him without pride, ego, greed or vanity. Put it into your own words (a prayer you could see yourself praying every day).

_____

_____

_____

_____

_____

_____

_____

_____

_____

_____

_____

_____

CHURCH CONNECTION

If you were in charge of training new volunteer leaders in your church, how would you communicate the idea of leadership in a way that empowers the volunteer, but also lets them know that they have responsibilities as well?

Pick a specific role in the church (e.g. greeters). How would want it explained to you? Do you think churches don't highlight the importance of volunteer leadership positions in the church because they are afraid of scaring people away? What can we do differently?

_____

_____

_____

_____

_____

_____

_____

_____

_____

_____

_____

_____

How can you (or how will you) find and ask someone younger to help you with what you are doing in church? How can you invest in others like others have invested in you?

_____

_____

_____

_____

_____

_____

_____

_____

_____

_____

_____

_____

_____

_____

_____

_____

BIGGER PICTURE

Next month is the due date for completion of your Released Projects. Some of you have already completed yours, while others are either presently implementing their project or will soon do so. Regardless, you have put a lot of time, energy, planning, and prayer into this project. But I hope you realize the role your mentor played in this process, and how their guidance and support helped you along in this journey.

In the space below, write down the ways your mentor has helped you with your Released Project since the beginning (be specific). Once you have finished your list, make sure you thank your mentor, mentioning those specific things.

_____

_____

_____

_____

_____

_____

_____

_____

_____

_____

_____

_____

CALLING AND VOCATION

Session Two

For we are God's handiwork, created in Christ Jesus to do good works, which God
prepared in advance for us to do.
(Ephesians 2:10)

One of the problems facing Christian teenagers is that a lot of Christian literature, sermons, and conversations deal with "calling"– the idea of a believer's God-given purpose in life. The issue, one I know many of you face (because your mentors and I faced it when we were your age), is that you may not know your calling right now. Nor are you expected to, for you will continue to grow in faith, knowledge, and maturity, and through those experiences God will reveal an "ever-weightier conviction" that will guide your life.

However, just because you may not have a definite "calling," does not mean that you cannot discern what God is inviting you into. We can discern this invitation through recognizing what spiritual gifts we may have. When we know and foster our spiritual gifts, we can utilize these gifts wherever we may be (job, location, situation, etc.). When we have this view, the goal is not to find an overarching "calling," but to recognize what God has given us to bless others, and daily being faithful in utilizing those gifts. It is my opinion that, when we are faithful in utilizing our gifts daily, we are living out God's ultimate calling for our lives.

In 1 Corinthians 12:12-27, Paul writes of the Church being like a body - every part is necessary and valuable. Here is a segment of that passage:

Suppose the foot says, "I am not a hand. So I don't belong to the body." By saying this, it cannot stop being part of the body. And suppose the ear says, "I am not an eye. So I don't belong to the body." By saying this, it cannot stop being part of the body. If the whole body were an eye, how could it hear? If the whole body were an ear, how could it smell? God has placed each part in the body just as he wanted it to be. If all the parts were the same, how could there be a body? As it is, there are many parts. But there is only one body."

These verses are important, for they help us realize that God has gifted so many people in so many ways - because every gift is necessary and valuable in its service to God, its use in the Church, and in its blessing of the world.

PERSONAL PRACTICE

What gifts has God given you so that you may bless others?

_____

_____

_____

_____

_____

_____

_____

Are you using these gifts? Why or why not?

_____

_____

_____

_____

_____

_____

_____

CHURCH CONNECTION

I want you to do a small exercise next time you attend Sunday worship at your church. From the moment you enter the parking lot, think about everything it takes for the church to function. Note each person who is serving (from the greeter at the door, to those on stage, sound people, etc.). How many different gifts are needed for church to be church on Sunday morning? Once you have a number, think about all the work that is done throughout the week for ministry to occur - how many gifts are necessary?

The point of this exercise is to recognize that Kaleo exists to help prepare you for Christian life and leadership, both inside and outside the church. God has gifted you to serve others. And while you may never be "on stage" at a church, I hope you recognize that your service is necessary, for church takes work - the harvest is plentiful, but the workers are few.

Write down all of the different tasks necessary for your church to function on Sunday. What is the grand total? During the week?

_____

_____

_____

_____

_____

_____

_____

_____

_____

Think about your answer to the first question (your gifts and whether or not you are using them). Now look at the list of gifts/people/tasks necessary for the Church to function on Sunday and during the week.

Is there a ministry/position/role in your church that aligns with your current gifting? If so, are you serving in that role? How would you go about learning more about or volunteering in that ministry – taking those faithful next steps?

_____

_____

_____

_____

_____

_____

_____

_____

_____

_____

_____

_____

_____

_____

BIGGER PICTURE

If you have not already, you will soon turn in your Released Project report. Congratulations! You put a lot of time, energy, and prayer into this project; I hope it has been a blessing to you as you have been a blessing to others.

There will be people who want to know about your project – how do you best communicate the project in clear, concise way? Use this space to practice a 1-2 sentence explanation of your project.

_____

_____

_____

_____

_____

_____

_____

_____

_____

_____

_____

_____

_____

_____

Looking back at the past year – write down your thoughts regarding the Released Project. Was a it a positive experience? What were some obstacles? What were some blessings/successes? What did you learn from this experience?

_____

_____

_____

_____

_____

_____

_____

_____

_____

_____

_____

_____

_____

_____

_____

_____

_____

_____

_____

_____

_____

_____

_____

_____

_____

_____

_____

_____

_____

_____

_____

_____

_____

_____

_____

_____

_____

MEMORIES AND BLESSINGS

NOTES

1. Max Carter, *Minutiae of the Meeting: Essays on Quaker Connections* (Greensboro: Guilford College, 1999), 14.

2. George Fox, *The Journal of George Fox*, ed. John Nickalls (Cambridge: Cambridge University Press, 1952), 9.

3. William Sewel, *The History of the Rise, Increase, and Progress of the Christian People Called Quakers, Intermixed with Several Remarkable Utterances*, vol. 1 (Philadelphia: Friends' Book Store, 1856), 327-328.

4. Rebecca Larson, *Daughters of Light: Quaker Women Preaching and Prophesying in the Colonies and Abroad, 1700-1775* (New York: Alfred A. Knopf, 1999), 4.

5. John Woolman, *The Journal and Major Essays of John Woolman*, ed. Phillips Moulton (Richmond: Friends United Press, 1989), 51.

6. Jared Diamond, *The World Until Yesterday: What Can We Learn from Traditional Societies* (New York: Penguin Books, 2012), 220.

7. Margaret Mead, *Culture and Commitment: A Study of the Generation Gap* (New York: Bodley Head, 1970), 128.

8. Lyle Dorsett, "Dwight L. Moody (1837–1899): Evangelist and Master Disciple Maker," *Knowing & Doing* (Fall 2011), 1.

9. Paul Dwight Moody & Arthur Percy Fitt, *The Shorter Life of D.L. Moody*, vol. 1 (Chicago: Bible Institute Colportage Association, 1900), 93.

10. Kara Powell, Jake Mulder & Brad Griffin, *Growing Young: Six Essential Strategies to Help Young People Discover and Love Your Church* (Grand Rapids: Baker Books, 2016), 53ff.

BIBLIOGRAPHY

Carter, Max. *Minutiae of the Meeting: Essays on Quaker Connections*. Greensboro: Guilford College, 1999.

Diamond, Jared. *The World Until Yesterday: What Can We Learn from Traditional Societies*. New York: Penguin Books, 2012.

Dorsett, Lyle. "Dwight L. Moody (1837–1899): Evangelist and Master Disciple Maker." *Knowing & Doing* (Fall 2011): 1.

Fox, George. *The Journal of George Fox*. Edited by John Nickalls. Cambridge: Cambridge University Press, 1952.

Larson, Rebecca. *Daughters of Light: Quaker Women Preaching and Prophesying in the Colonies and Abroad, 1700-1775*. New York: Alfred A. Knopf, 1999.

Mead, Margaret. *Culture and Commitment: A Study of the Generation Gap*. New York: Bodley Head, 1970.

Moody, Paul Dwight & Arthur Percy Fitt. *The Shorter Life of D.L. Moody*. Vol. 1. Chicago: Bible Institute Colportage Association, 1900.

Powell, Kara, Jake Mulder & Brad Griffin. *Growing Young: Six Essential Strategies to Help Young People Discover and Love Your Church*. Grand Rapids: Baker Books, 2016.

Sewel, William. *The History of the Rise, Increase, and Progress of the Christian People Called Quakers, Intermixed with Several Remarkable Utterances*. Vol. 1. Philadelphia: Friends' Book Store, 1856.

Woolman, John. *The Journal and Major Essays of John Woolman*. Edited by Phillips Moulton. Richmond: Friends United Press, 1989.

ABOUT THE AUTHOR

Derek Brown is Professor of Pastoral Ministry and Chair of the Pastoral Ministry department at Barclay College, where he also serves as College Chaplain, and Director of the Master of Arts in Pastoral Ministry and the Master of Arts in Transformational Leadership. In addition to his credentials in theology, biblical studies, and ecclesiology, Derek is also a scholar of organizational and leadership theory. While his main research focus is Quaker pastoral theology and ecclesiology, he also enjoys researching the broader interplay of theology and culture, as well as the growing field of leadership studies. Derek lives in Haviland, KS with his wife, Jessica, and his twin daughters, Sophia and Sarah.